FRANCE
the land

Greg Nickles

A Bobbie Kalman Book
The Lands, Peoples, and Cultures Series

 Crabtree Publishing Company

The Lands, Peoples, and Cultures Series
Created by Bobbie Kalman

Coordinating editor
Ellen Rodger

Project development, editing, and photo research
First Folio Resource Group, Inc.
  Pauline Beggs
  Tom Dart
  Bruce Krever
  Kathryn Lane
  Debbie Smith

Design
David Vereschagin/Quadrat Communications

Separations and film
Embassy Graphics

Printer
Dot 'n Line Image Inc.

Consultants
Thérèse Sabaryn, University of Waterloo;
Daphnée Saurel

Photographs
AP/Wide World Photos: p. 29 (top); Yann Arthus-Bertrand/Altitude/Photo Researchers: p. 19 (bottom), p. 28; Christophe Bluntzer/Impact: p. 22 (bottom), p. 26 (bottom); Peter Crabtree: title page, p.13 (bottom), p. 15 (top), (bottom); Corbis/Dave Bartruff: p. 12 (top); Corbis/Jack Fields: p. 18 (bottom); Corbis/Laurence Fordyce/Eye Ubiquitous: p. 10 (top); Corbis/Owen Franken: p. 20 (bottom right); Corbis/Franz-Marc Frei: p. 17 (bottom); Corbis/John Heseltine: p. 20 (left); Corbis/Robert Holmes: p. 29 (bottom); Corbis/ Wolfgang Kaehler: p. 11 (right); Corbis/Catherine Karnow: p. 16 (bottom); Corbis/ Charles and Josette Lenars: p. 12 (bottom); Corbis/ Ludovic Maisant: p. 16 (top); Corbis/ Stephanie Maze: p. 14 (bottom); Corbis/ Photo B.D.V.: p. 22 (left); Corbis/Bryan Pickering/Eye Ubiquitous: p. 5 (top); Corbis/The Purcell Team: p. 14 (top); Corbis/ Hubert Stadler: p. 10 (bottom); Corbis/ Karl Weatherly: p. 13 (top); Corbis/Adam Woolfitt: p. 9 (right), p. 17 (top); Art Brewer/International Stock: p. 11 (bottom); Victor Englebert/Photo Researchers: p. 4, p. 27 (bottom); G. Fontaine/ Publiphoto/Photo Researchers: p. 25; George Gerster/Photo Researchers: p. 7; Sylvain Grandadam/Photo Researchers: p. 31 (top); Groenendyk/Photo Researchers: p. 6 (bottom); George Haling/Photo Researchers: p. 5 (bottom); Tim Holt/Photo Researchers: p. 24 (top left); H. Hughes/ Visa/Impact: p. 18 (top); Huron/Editing/Impact: p. 21 (bottom); Francis Jalain/Explorer/Photo Researchers: p. 23 (top), p. 27 (top); Ronny Jaques/Photo Researchers: title page; Gordon Johnson/Photo Researchers: p. 11 (left); Greg Johnston/International Stock Photo: p. 8 (bottom); Alain Le Garsmeur/ Impact: contents page; Rene Mattes Explorer/ Photo Researchers: p. 25 (bottom); Tom McHugh/ Photo Researchers: p. 31 (bottom left and bottom right); Peter Miller/Photo Researchers: p. 8 (top); Nieto/Jerrican/Photo Researchers: p. 23 (bottom); Jean-Pierre Nacivet/Explorer/Photo Researchers: cover; Porterfield/Chickering/Photo Researchers: p. 6 (top); Reuters/Jacky Naegelen/Archive Photos: p. 24 (top right); Eric A. Soder/Photo Researchers: p. 30; Stockman/ International Stock Photo: p. 5 (middle); p. 9 (left), p. 26 (top); Ulrike Welsch/Photo Researchers: p. 20 (top right); Brent Winebrenner/ International Stock Photo: p. 19 (top), p. 21 (top)

Map
Jim Chernishenko

Illustrations
David Wysotski, Allure Illustrations: back cover

Cover: The 300-meter (984-foot) Eiffel Tower was built for the 1889 Paris Exhibition.

Title page: Rows of grape vines lead up to the chateau of the company that makes the red wine of the Burgundy region.

Icon: Grapes, a common crop that is fermented to make wine, appear at the head of each section.

Back cover: Gothic cathedrals such as Notre Dame are decorated with grotesque ornamental figures called gargoyles.

Published by
Crabtree Publishing Company

PMB 16A
350 Fifth Avenue
Suite 3308
New York
N.Y. 10118

612 Welland Avenue
St. Catharines
Ontario, Canada
L2M 5V6

73 Lime Walk
Headington
Oxford OX3 7AD
United Kingdom

Cataloging in Publication Data
Nickles, Greg, 1969
    France, the land / Greg Nickles
        p.cm.-- (The lands, peoples, and cultures series)
    "A Bobbie Kalman book."
    Includes index
    Summary: Explores the beauty of France, its major cities, and its overseas departments.
    ISBN 0-86505-321-9 (paper) -- ISBN 0-86505-241-7 (rlb.)
        1. France--Description and travel--Juvenile literature. [1. France--Description and travel.] I. Title. II Series.
    DC17.N52 2000
    j944   LC 00-026067
                                                             CIP

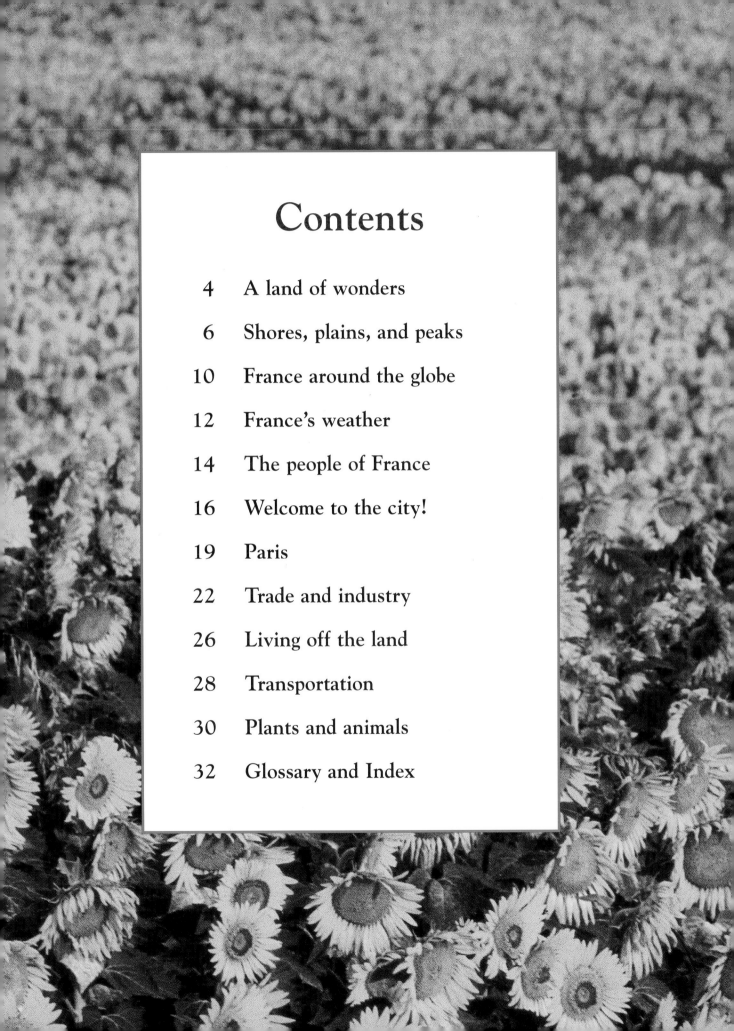

Contents

A land of wonders

France is a land of many wonders. One of the largest and oldest countries in Europe, it is known for its great cities, majestic mountains, quiet countryside, and long stretches of beaches.

All over the world

France's modern industries have influenced life around the world. Many people drive French cars and use technology developed by France's rail, air, and space industries. They wear clothing created by French fashion designers and perfumes made from France's flowers. They also eat delicious French cuisine, or fine cooking, and drink French wines.

Facts at a glance

Official name: *République Française* (Republic of France)
Area: 551,500 square kilometers (212,935 square miles), not including overseas holdings
Population: 58,500,000
Capital city: Paris
Official language: French
Main religion: Roman Catholic Church
National holiday: Bastille Day, July 14

Waves crashing against the cliffs at Étretat, on the north Atlantic coast, created this arch which looks like an elephant with a large trunk.

(above) The **château**, *or castle, of Saumur was built on top of an ancient fortress. It overlooks the Loire Valley.*

(right) The old village of Saint-Montant has narrow cobblestone streets that no car could fit through.

(below) The village of Gordes is perched on the edge of the high Vaucluse Plateau in southeastern France. The buildings, including a twelfth-century castle, are made from a beige stone that appears orange in the early morning sun.

 # Shores, plains, and peaks

France is known for its wide variety of landscapes. There are plains, which are flat meadowlands, and rocky shores in the north; highlands, or rugged hills, in the center; mountains and sunny beaches in the south, and an island in the Mediterranean Sea.

Fertile valleys

Many rivers flow through France. Over millions of years, France's five major rivers — the Loire, Seine, Rhône, Garonne, and Rhine — carved broad river valleys into the land. People built towns and cities in these river valleys, where they farmed the **fertile** soil and used the rivers for transportation and trade.

Rocky and rugged

The coastline in northwest France is dominated by **granite** and **limestone** cliffs, with ports and fishing villages below. High tides wash in and out along the shore. Inland, the ground is mostly ancient rock, worn away by the weather and thinly covered with soil. There are also many moors, or hilly marshes. In the country's northeast, the low Ardennes and Vosges Mountains cross the land, their slopes covered with forests and farmland.

Gentle plains

Northern and western France is covered by plains, which are often broken up by woods and rolling hills. These plains stretch westward to the Atlantic coast, with its wide beaches, dense pine forests, and **sand dunes**. At about 3 kilometers (2 miles) long and 115 meters (375 feet) high, the great Dune du Pilat is the largest sand dune in Europe. In the midst of France's northern plains sits Île de France, or "Island of France." Île de France is not really an island, but a huge, dish-like **depression** in the land. Île de France is also called the Paris Basin because it is home to the city of Paris.

(top) Visitors look for crabs and lobsters among the rocks in the Bay of Biscay.

(below) The village of Les Andelys lies on the banks of the winding Seine River.

Mysterious megaliths

Thousands of years ago, ancient peoples in France constructed megaliths, or huge monuments made of stones. They are found mostly in the northwest, in places such as Carnac. Menhirs are the most common type of megalith. Tall stones are placed beside one another to form lines, circles, or other patterns. Over 1000 menhirs stand in the fields of Menec, in Carnac, in rows that are each more than 1 kilometer (.6 miles) long.

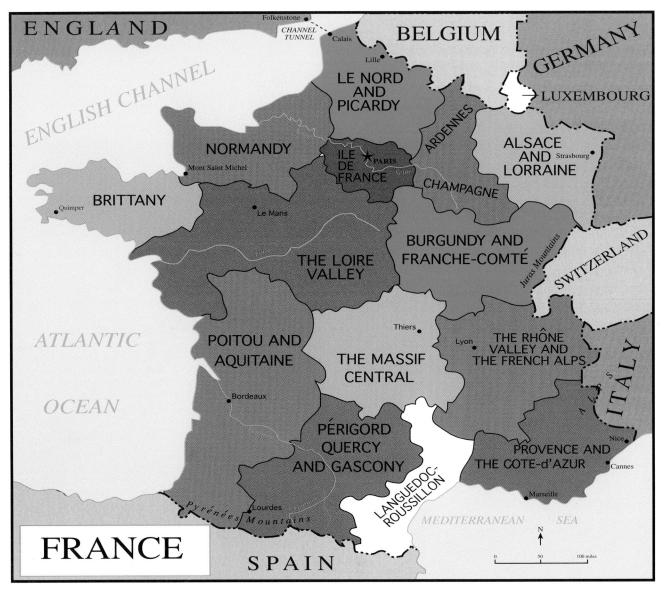

ENGLAND

Folkenstone

CHANNEL TUNNEL

Calais

BELGIUM

GERMANY

Lille

ENGLISH CHANNEL

LE NORD AND PICARDY

LUXEMBOURG

NORMANDY

ARDENNES

ALSACE AND LORRAINE

Strasbourg

Mont Saint Michel

ILE DE FRANCE

PARIS

Seine

BRITTANY

Quimper

CHAMPAGNE

Le Mans

THE LOIRE VALLEY

BURGUNDY AND FRANCHE-COMTÉ

Jura Mountains

SWITZERLAND

ATLANTIC OCEAN

POITOU AND AQUITAINE

THE MASSIF CENTRAL

Thiers

Lyon

THE RHÔNE VALLEY AND THE FRENCH ALPS

ITALY

ALPS

Bordeaux

Nice

PÉRIGORD QUERCY AND GASCONY

LANGUEDOC-ROUSSILLON

PROVENCE AND THE CÔTE-d'AZUR

Cannes

Lourdes

Pyrénées Mountains

Marseille

MEDITERRANEAN SEA

N

FRANCE

SPAIN

0   50   100 miles

At 4807 meters (15,800 feet), Mont Blanc, in the French Alps, is the highest peak in Europe.

The Massif Central

The Massif Central, in the center of France, is a large, wild region of highlands. Many were once the peaks and cones of volcanoes. Over time, wind and rain **eroded** the volcanoes, and water filled some of their huge craters to form lakes. The dramatic **gorges** of the Tarn River cut through the region's major chain of ancient mountains, the Cévennes. The many hot springs in this area are favorite tourist attractions. Few people live in the Massif Central, however, because the land is too rough and the soil too thin to support much farming. Only a few homes, often built from the local dark, volcanic stone, are found on the highlands.

Mega mountains

Tall mountains stand in the east and southwest parts of France. The Jura Mountains and French Alps, in the east, are two of the most jagged and majestic mountain chains in the world. Hundreds of years ago, some people thought these misty, fairy-tale-like peaks were the homes of angels. Today, tourists visit this region's well-known ski resorts and spas.

The Pyrénées chain in the southwest rises high from the surrounding plains, separating France and its neighbor, Spain. One of the most famous breaches, or openings, in this mountain barrier is the narrow Brèche de Roland. It is named after Roland, a legendary hero who is said to have died there defending France from **invaders**.

After stopping to graze, herds of sheep wander down a road in the Pyrénées Mountains.

On the coasts

France's bright, warm south has been made famous by artists such as Paul Cézanne and Vincent Van Gogh. They captured the region's rich sunlight and colorful farmland in their paintings. One of the most popular areas is the Riviera, on the Mediterranean coast, which is famous for its luxurious resorts and beaches. The Riviera is also known as the Côte d'Azur, or the "sky-blue coast," because of its brilliant blue water. Biarritz, on the Atlantic coast, is another popular spot for people who enjoy going to the beach.

(below) Sunbathers enjoy the warm weather in Biarritz.

(above) On the southern tip of Corsica, the old walled town of Bonifacio is perched high above the harbor.

The island of Corsica

Corsica lies in the Mediterranean Sea about 160 kilometers (100 miles) south of France and 80 kilometers (50 miles) west of Italy. Corsica is dry and rugged, with rocky cliffs, mountains, and deep valleys. About one-quarter of its interior is covered with a dense undergrowth called *maquis*. The *maquis* is made up of sweet-smelling shrubs, such as white heather, that wind their way around trees. Between April and June each year, masses of the heather bloom, an event called the "white spring."

France around the globe

Houses built on stilts stand among palm trees in the village of Saint Laurent, in French Guiana.

France's territory stretches around the globe. Until the mid-1700s, France ruled an **empire** that included Louisiana, Quebec, and other parts of North America. From the late 1800s until the mid-1900s, it also ruled **colonies** in Africa, the Middle East, and East Asia. France's overseas holdings of today are colonies that remained under France's control after its empire broke up.

Overseas holdings

French Guiana, in the northeast part of South America, is the largest of France's overseas holdings. Dense rainforests cover much of the hot, humid land, while small towns dot the coastline. Most of France's other overseas holdings are islands, including Guadeloupe and Martinique in the Caribbean, Saint Pierre and Miquelon off the eastern coast of Canada, Mayotte and Réunion in the Indian Ocean, and Tahiti and the 129 other islands that make up the territory of French Polynesia.

Houses and fields cling to a hillside below a flat-topped mountain in Réunion.

(left) Fishers haul in their catches at the village of Les Anses d'Arlets on the Caribbean island of Martinique.

(middle) Boys walk down a street on the North Atlantic island of Saint Pierre.

(bottom) A sunny cove on the island of Moorea. France claims 129 islands in French Polynesia.

Changing relationships

There have been many changes in France's overseas lands in the past 30 years. For example, in 1998, New Caledonia, in the southwest Pacific, voted to become independent. This decision followed fighting in the late 1980s between the Kanaks, New Caledonia's native-born people, and the French. In the future, people in other overseas lands may ask for their independence as well.

France's weather

France's weather varies depending on the region. The Atlantic coast is affected by the Gulf Stream, a **current** of warm water that takes the chill off winter temperatures and moistens and cools summer air. The country's eastern border is affected by cold winds from Eastern Europe. Temperatures are also cooler in the mountains.

The stormy coasts

France's north and west coasts are much wetter than the rest of the country because they are exposed to the moisture-rich winds from the ocean. In these areas, it is common for a light, misty rain to fall about 200 days each year. The region of Brittany, in the far northwest, is the wettest and stormiest part of the country. Fierce winds, especially during winter, cause high waves to smash into the rocky coast.

A man closes his umbrella as a rare rainstorm brews over a beach in Saint Tropez, in the south of France.

The sunny southeast

The French Alps shield southeast France from cold winds and rain. Instead, the land is warmed by the breezes of the Mediterranean Sea. Winter is marked by occasional short, heavy rainstorms. Summer is hot and rain may not fall for up to two months at a time. These conditions sometimes cause a drought, a period when crops and other plants do not get enough water to survive. During times of drought, fires break out in areas of dried-out forest and scrub.

A woman gets caught in the rain on her way home from work.

Skiers glide through deep powder snow in the cloudy French Alps.

Mountain weather

France's mountains receive more heavy rain and snow than the rest of the country. In fact, many mountain tops are covered in snow year-round. In the winter, the peak of Mont Blanc can receive up to 47 meters (154 feet) of snow! High in these mountains sit glaciers, huge rivers of ice formed by layer upon layer of packed-down snow. You can ski down the glaciers in both the winter and summer!

Mistral menace

In the winter and spring, low-lying areas in the south of France are sometimes bothered by a swirling, cold, dry wind called the *mistral*. The *mistral* blows down the Rhône River Valley from the Massif Central at speeds that can reach 200 kilometers (124 miles) per hour. This bitter wind sometimes rages for up to four days in a row. It can ruin crops and buildings, and blow down trees.

A postman delivers the mail on bicycle in Avignon in the south of France.

The French are known for their love of life, food, and art. Whether they live in the cities or the countryside, they share a strong pride in their country, achievements, and way of life.

French ancestry

The French come from many backgrounds. Most are the **descendants** of peoples, such as the Celts, Romans, and Vikings, who came to France from other parts of Europe centuries ago. These people became deeply attached to the regions in which they lived. Over time, each region developed its own customs, traditions, dress, and language that were very different from those in the rest of France. Even today, some people in these regions still live a traditional way of life.

(right) A farmer from Burgundy stands in his vineyard. Like many Burgundians, he continues the region's ancient tradition of grape growing and wine making.

(top) On the shore of a canal, a man and woman heave a huge lever to open a lock, which controls the level of the canal's water.

Immigrants

Throughout the nineteenth and early twentieth centuries, France became home to immigrants from countries such as Spain, Italy, Portugal, and Turkey. More recent immigrants have come from France's former colonies in Southeast Asia, such as Vietnam, and in North Africa, especially Algeria and Morocco.

Although most immigrants have lived in France for years and are now French citizens, they have had a hard time being accepted as equals. Many immigrants have little money and cannot find good jobs or comfortable housing. To help ease this problem, many French are fighting **racism** in their communities.

Parisians stroll down steps on the banks of the Seine River. Some have their portraits drawn by artists.

A hurdy-gurdy player sets up his organ in front of the Pompidou Center.

Welcome to the city!

France's major cities, such as Paris, Lyon, Marseille, and Nice, are filled with great monuments and interesting buildings. They are also famous for their fun night life, spectacular museums and art galleries, charming cafés, and large, outdoor food markets.

Ancient roots

The centers of many French cities are very old, often dating back over 2000 years. The ruins of **temples**, arenas, **aqueducts**, and other ancient structures are reminders of a rich past. Large, beautiful cathedrals built many centuries ago still stand. Narrow cobblestone streets wind between old houses, apartments, and shops. To protect their historic centers, some French cities have passed laws to limit new construction in the area and to ban cars.

(right) **The tower of the town hall is visible just beyond the old buildings of Lille's city center.**

(below) **Bullfights are still held in an ancient Roman arena, in Nîmes, in southeast France.**

The Saône River is one of two rivers that runs through Lyon.

Bon appétit in Lyon

Lyon became known in the 1500s as a center of silk manufacturing. At the time, silk was very rare and expensive. People built *traboules*, or covered passageways, to protect the fabric from the weather as it was moved from place to place. Some *traboules* can still be found among the alleyways in the old section of Lyon. Still a center for the **textile** industry, Lyon is also a major banking and pharmaceutical, or drug-manufacturing, city. It is most famous, however, as one of the best places in France for fine food. The farmland around Lyon produces the country's greatest variety of fresh food, and Lyon's streets teem with small restaurants called *bouchons* where you can eat Lyon specialties.

Cafés line the sidewalk in front of colorfully timbered buildings in the city of Rouen.

(above) The Promenade des Anglais, a busy street that is home to many luxurious apartment buildings, hotels, and stores, runs along the beach in Nice.

(left) One of Marseille's best-known attractions is its noisy fish market, where vendors sell fresh seafood caught by local fishers.

Sunny Marseille

Ancient Greeks founded Marseille, France's oldest city, over 2500 years ago. Then, Romans, who once ruled a huge empire that included France, developed it into a successful trading port. Today, Marseille is France's major seaport and a center of shipbuilding.

Glamorous Nice

Founded over 2000 years ago as a Greek colony, Nice is the largest city on the Riviera. Its beaches and fun atmosphere attract vacationers year-round. The old part of the city is filled with narrow buildings, winding streets, colorful food and flower markets, and many restaurants, art galleries, and shops. The highlight of Nice's year is the two-week-long Mardi Gras Carnival in February, with parades, music, fireworks, and large street parties.

Paris

Paris, France's bustling **capital**, lies on the banks of the Seine River. Over the centuries, Paris has been home to many famous rulers, artists, and great thinkers. Today, it is the country's center of politics, business, and culture.

Back in time

Paris was first settled about 2200 years ago by an ancient people called the Parisii. They built their town on a long, boat-shaped island, now called Île de la Cité, in the middle of the Seine River. Later taken over by the ancient Romans and other peoples, the town spread beyond the island to the banks of the Seine.

The lay of the land

Today, Paris is a sprawling city that continues to grow out from its ancient center. The oldest section includes Île de la Cité and the Seine's Right and Left Banks. Many of the city's big businesses are on the Right Bank, while scholars, artists, writers, and craftspeople live on the Left Bank. The Left Bank is also home to France's oldest university, the Sorbonne.

Bridges crossing over the Seine connect Île de la Cité and Île Saint-Louis with the Left and Right Banks in Paris.

Beyond the old city

A busy road encircles the old city. It was built along the former path of Paris's city walls, which once protected its people from invaders. Beyond this road lies the huge, modern section of Paris and the majority of its industries, apartments, offices, and other buildings. Most Parisians live in this part of the city and in large, new **suburbs** that have sprung up around Paris.

A man reads a newspaper in a café on the Left Bank.

The Eiffel Tower

The unmistakable Eiffel Tower is Paris's best-known landmark. It was designed by Gustave Eiffel, a French **engineer**. When it was completed in 1889, this structure was the world's tallest building. Although the tower was meant to be temporary, it was never demolished. Today, it houses restaurants, radio and television transmitters, a post office, and a museum. Each year, millions of tourists climb its 1652 steps or ride up its 100-year-old elevator for a view of the city.

(below) The Eiffel Tower's iron girders, or supports, help keep the structure steady in windy weather.

(above) The sculptures in Jean Tinguelay's fountain outside the Pompidou Center spin and spray water.

(below) Rooftops seem to overlap in this crowded Paris neighborhood.

Shoppers, cars, and cafés crowd Les Champs Élysées, a tree-lined boulevard in Paris.

Along the Champs Élysées

The Champs Élysées, in the old city, is the best-known street in Paris. Constantly streaming with traffic, this grand **boulevard** is lined with monuments, gardens, cafés, movie theaters, museums, and stylish clothing stores. The Élysée palace, home of France's president, is also on this street.

Home of the arts

Paris is a busy place for music, dance, drama, and art. The grand Louvre museum, which was once a royal palace, is one of the world's finest museums. It holds a huge collection of ancient Egyptian, Greek, and Roman works; sculptures by artists such as Rodin and Michelangelo; and canvases by almost every famous painter, including *Mona Lisa* by Leonardo da Vinci. Other important art galleries include the Pompidou Center; the Musée d'Orsay, a renovated train station that displays paintings by France's best-known artists; and the Musée en Herbe, a children's museum.

You can see the centuries-old Louvre through the new glass and steel pyramid, which is the museum's main entrance.

France manufactures many products that are famous around the world, such as Michelin tires, Citroën automobiles, and Limoges china. France is also known for the fine foods, wines, fashions, and perfumes that it produces.

Fine fashion

Fashion has long been one of France's best-known exports. An Englishman named Charles Frederick Worth started the modern fashion industry in Paris during the 1800s. His company designed *haute couture*, or expensive one-of-a-kind clothes, which he presented in exciting fashion shows. The fashion houses of Paris still create *haute couture* by famous designers such as Kenzo and Jean-Paul Gaulthier. Many also make popular *prêt-à-porter*, or "ready-to-wear," pieces that are mass-produced and more affordable. The latest styles are previewed each spring and autumn in stunning shows held in Paris.

(left) A model walks down the runway at Jean-Paul Gaulthier's show of spring and summer fashions.

(below) A huge car lot filled with Citroëns lies beside the factory in Aulnay, in western France.

Fancy fragrances

France's perfume industry dates back to the 1500s. At that time, fragrances were made for **aristocrats** and other wealthy people who could afford them. The perfumes were made mostly from flowers grown in Grasse, in southern France. It took until the 1920s for perfumes to become widely popular, after famous fashion designers such as Coco Chanel lent their names to special brands. Today, perfumes are still made from France's huge crops of orange blossoms, lilies of the valley, jasmine, carnations, and lavender. These ingredients are expensive, however, so chemicals and plant and animal **extracts** are also used.

High-tech and old-fashioned

Among France's most important industries are **high-tech** fields, such as space travel and **nuclear power**, and the tourism, banking, health care, and chemical industries. Many of these industries are based in cities, but some small towns are also manufacturing centers. For generations, the people there have specialized in making one product. For example, the town of Thiers is nicknamed the "Capital of Cutlery" because its residents have been creating knives and other cutting tools for 1500 years.

A crystal maker in the city of St. Louis, in northeast France, grinds a vase.

Workers at a perfume factory pour rose petals, which will be used to make a new fragrance, into a large vat.

(below) The cone-shaped nose of the Concorde jet tilts downward during takeoff and landing so that pilots can see the runway better.

Up and away

France's aeronautics, or air travel, industry has built many helicopters, jet fighters, and **missiles**. In cooperation with England and other European countries, it has produced swift passenger airliners such as the supersonic Concorde. Traveling faster than the speed of sound, at about 2100 kilometers (1300 miles) per hour, Concordes whisk passengers between destinations such as Paris, New York, and London, England in a fraction of the time it takes ordinary planes.

France in space

As a member of the European Space Agency (ESA), France manufactures high-tech equipment for space exploration. Under France's leadership, the ESA builds and launches Ariane rockets, which send **satellites** into orbit. The ESA is also helping the United States, Russia, Canada, and other nations build the new International Space Station.

The Ariane 5 rocket lifts off from its launching pad in French Guiana.

The European Union

The European Union (EU) is an organization of fifteen European countries, including France, England, Germany, Italy, Ireland, and Spain. Members of the EU work together to promote trade among themselves and with the rest of the world. In early 1999, the EU introduced the eurodollar, a new **currency** that replaces each country's own currency. The new common currency is one way to bring together the economies of the EU's members.

A nuclear power plant provides energy to people living in the Loire Valley.

Harnessing nuclear power

France's industries need a lot of electricity to operate their high-tech machinery. Since France has few deposits of oil, coal, and natural gas, it has developed its own sources of energy in the last few decades. Today, up to three-quarters of the country's electricity — the highest proportion of any country in the world — is generated by nuclear power plants. The government has been very careful to make its nuclear plants safe, but some people oppose them. They wonder how the government will dispose of large amounts of radioactive waste, a deadly **byproduct** of the plants. They also fear that this waste might spill into the environment by accident, seriously harming people and animals.

More power

In addition to nuclear power, the French have experimented with water power in the mountainous south and **solar power** in the Pyrénées. They also built the world's first tidal power plant, where the rising and falling tide waters turn the plant's turbines, or motors, creating electricity.

The changing economy

Before World War II (1939–45) devastated many parts of France, most people worked on farms or in small businesses. After the war, the government rebuilt the country with modern mining, iron, and steel businesses, and with high-tech industries. For the three decades after the war, now called the *Trentes Glorieuses*, or "Glorious Thirty," almost everyone had a job.

Since 1974, however, French workers have faced many challenges. Other countries began producing goods such as coal, steel, fabrics, and ships less expensively than France. Many French companies were driven out of business. Changes to factory work, such as using computers and industrial robots, also cost many jobs. Although high unemployment is still a problem today, the government hopes that the European Union will create many new businesses and jobs.

Living off the land

France is a world leader in **agriculture**. Farmers grow a wide variety of fruit, vegetables, and grains, and raise all sorts of **livestock** for their meat and milk. In addition, fishers catch huge quantities of seafood which are enjoyed by people around the country.

Northern crops

The largest and most fertile region for farming is in France's northern half. Sugar beets and cereals such as wheat, corn, and barley grow in the large, open fields of the Paris Basin. The damp, cooler northwest is an ideal place for growing apples and potatoes.

Southern harvests

Many types of fruit and vegetables grow in France's drier, sunny south. Grapes are one of the country's most important crops. White wine, red wine, and bubbly **champagne** are all made from different types of grapes. Other fruit grown in the south include peaches, cherries, nectarines, apricots, kiwis, and olives. While many crops are harvested with modern equipment, most soft fruits are still picked by hand to prevent bruising.

(above) Fields of lavender stretch as far as the eye can see.

(below) Farmers use pitchforks to load cabbages into a wagon.

Two men make sure that their pig does not gobble up the very rare truffles that it finds.

"Black diamonds"

Truffles, which are small, round mushrooms about the size of golf balls, are an expensive **delicacy** with a nutty flavor. They grow wild underground in the woods of France, usually by the roots of hazelnut or oak trees. Truffles are called "black diamonds" because they are very rare and valuable. They are so hard to find that, during truffle season in the winter, some people use trained pigs to sniff out their location. Once dug up and cleaned, people cook and eat truffles whole or chopped up in other foods.

On the seas

The French enjoy many kinds of seafood, hauled in daily by the country's thousands of fishing boats. Most French boats fish in nearby waters, such as the Atlantic Ocean and English Channel, but some vessels also visit the waters off the coasts of Newfoundland and Iceland. Catches in these areas include sole and tuna. The Mediterranean Sea is a source of sardines and shellfish such as lobsters and crabs. Freshwater fish, such as trout and pike, are caught in the country's rivers and streams.

Fishing boats prepare to unload their huge catches of crabs.

Transportation

France's transportation system is fast and efficient. Cars, trucks, planes, boats, and trains carry goods and passengers around the country and around the world.

Behind the wheel

The French love to drive. Each day, millions of cars and transport trucks speed along the country's *autoroutes*, or highways, that join major cities. France's smaller towns are linked by narrow, winding roads on which drivers travel much slower. People also tend to drive slowly in cities because the traffic is so heavy! To help ease the congestion, some major intersections do not have traffic lights. Instead, cars and trucks drive counter-clockwise around traffic circles until they reach the street where they want to turn.

Twelve streets radiate out from the traffic circle around the Arc de Triomphe. This 50-meter (164-foot) arch was completed in 1836 to honor the military victories of the great French emperor Napoleon Bonaparte.

By rail

Train travel is very popular in France. Since 1981, the world's fastest regular passenger trains, called TGVs, have connected France's major cities. TGV stands for *train à grande vitesse*, or high-speed train. Today, the TGVs, which can zoom along at 300 kilometers (186 miles) per hour, connect some 50 French cities and also run to England and other neighboring countries.

The Channel Tunnel

The Channel Tunnel, also known as the Chunnel, is an undersea tunnel that links Calais, France, to Folkestone, England. Completed in 1994, it is one of the greatest engineering marvels in the world. The Chunnel stretches for an amazing 50 kilometers (30 miles) underneath the English Channel. Inside are two rail lines, one for trains traveling to France and the other for trains traveling to England, with a service tunnel in between. The high-speed Eurostar trains carry goods, passengers, and vehicles from one country to the next.

(above) A highspeed Eurostar train emerges from the Chunnel in Calais, France.

*(left) Riders on Paris's huge underground subway system, the **Métro**, consult a map outside a station.*

Boring through the earth

People first began talking about an undersea tunnel linking France with England in 1751, but no one wanted to undertake such a dangerous and expensive project. It was not until 1986 that the French and British governments agreed to begin the difficult construction job. Over the next several years, crews used enormous, specially made machines to **bore** through solid rock, far beneath the seabed of the English Channel. Then, they lined the tunnel with concrete. When the Chunnel was completed, people could take a train underneath the English Channel instead of flying or traveling by ferry.

Plants and animals

Many different plants and animals live in France. Large forests of pine, oak, and chestnut trees stand in the Massif Central and on mountain slopes in the south. France's countryside is covered with long grasses and colorful wildflowers, such as red summer poppies and blue cornflowers. Here, bats, foxes, and hares live among more unusual species such as wild boars and black bulls.

Really wild animals

France's large wild boars can be extremely fierce creatures. These animals, which are the **ancestors** of common farm hogs, often use their powerful tusks as weapons. The remote parts of the Pyrénées are home to the bearded vulture. If this rare bird is flying overhead, watch out! It is known for dropping bones from the air onto the ground in order to break them and take out the **marrow**, its favorite food.

The Camargue

One of the most stunning wildlife areas in France is a **nature reserve** called the Camargue. The Camargue is a large river delta, or area of flat, marshy fields and shallow lakes, located in Provence. It often seems peaceful and deserted, but in fact it teems with insects, amphibians, birds, and other animals. Amidst its tall rushes and grass, **cicadas** buzz, bees hum, and fish splash in the water.

Pretty in pink

About 300 kinds of birds can be found in the Camargue, including great flocks of seagulls and long-legged storks. The most striking birds are the brilliant pink flamingoes. They wade slowly through the water on their stilt-like legs, craning their long necks to scoop up food in their bent bills.

The Camargue is the only place in Europe where flamingoes live.

A gardian herds Camargue horses, whose broad hooves are well-suited to the marshlands where they live.

France's cowhands

The Camargue is also home to black bulls and stocky white horses that feed on the Camargue's grasses. The bulls are raised and herded by rugged *gardians*. Mounted on horses and clad in jeans, jackets, and wide-brimmed hats, the *gardians* look much like North American cowboys. They breed the black cattle for the bullring or sell them for beef, and they herd the white horses for work animals.

Protecting wildlife

For many years, the French expanded their cities and industries without giving much thought to the effect on the environment. Marshes were drained, trees were cut, and factories polluted the air and water. Today, people are trying to correct this damage and preserve the environment. They have established national parks and nature reserves, such as the Camargue, and passed laws to protect animals such as eagles, wolves, and bears. The government has also funded programs to reintroduce animals that have almost disappeared, such as the griffon vulture.

(above) A wild boar nurses her young.

(left) Rare chamois mountain goats live in pastures and rocky areas of the French Alps.

31

# Glossary

agriculture The practice or science of farming

ancestor An earlier type of animal from which another type of animal is descended

aqueduct A bridge-like structure with a long pipe that brings water from far away

aristocrat A noble or member of the upper class

bore To drill

boulevard A wide street

byproduct Something that is produced from something else that is made

capital A city where the government of a state or country is located

champagne A bubbly wine made in the region of Champagne, in France, which people often drink for celebrations

cicada An insect with two pairs of transparent wings that is known for the male's buzzing sound

colony An area controlled by a distant country

currency Money

current The flow of water along a path in the ocean

delicacy A fine food

depression An area that is lower than the surrounding area

descendant A person who can trace his or her family roots to a certain family or group

empire A group of countries under one ruler or government

engineer A person who uses science to design and build structures and machines

erode To wear away gradually, as with wind and rain wearing away mountain peaks

extract A concentrated preparation

fertile Able to produce abundant crops or vegetation

gorge A deep, narrow, rocky valley

granite A type of rock that is very hard

high-tech Using advanced, modern technology

invader A person who enters with force

limestone A rock used for building that is easy to carve

livestock Farm animals

marrow The tissue inside bones

missile A weapon that is fired at a target

nature reserve A park where wildlife is protected from hunters and is observed by scientists and tourists

nuclear power Electricity generated from the energy that is created when atoms come together or split apart

racism The act of treating someone unfairly based on one's ethnic group

sand dune A mound of sand formed by the wind

satellite A man-made object that revolves around the earth or other bodies in space

solar power Electricity generated from sunlight

suburb A neighborhood on the edge of a city

temple A building used for religious services

textile A fabric or cloth

vineyard An orchard where grapes are grown to make wine

 # Index

1 2 3 4 5 6 7 8 9 0 Printed in the USA 5 4 3 2 1 0